TULSA CITY-COUNTY LIBRARY

JKJC

Measure It with Math!

MEASURING VOLUME

Anne O'Daly

PowerKiDS press

Published in 2024 by The Rosen Publishing Group, Inc.
2544 Clinton Street, Buffalo, NY 14224

Copyright © 2023 Brown Bear Books Ltd

All rights reserved. No part of this book may be reproduced in any form without permission in writing from the publisher, except by a reviewer.

Portions of this work were originally authored by Chris Woodford and published as *Volume*. All new material this edition authored by Anne O'Daly.

Children's Publisher: Anne O'Daly
Design Manager: Keith Davis
Picture Manager: Sophie Mortimer

Picture credits:
Key: t = top, tr = top right, b = bottom
Front Cover: Shutterstock: Africa Studio tr, Miguel Guasch Fuxa l, New Africa tl, Frederico Rostagno r.
Interior: Dreamstime: Robyn Mackenzie 28cl; Shutterstock: Africa Studio 13, Necula Valentin Andrei 5b, Max Dallocco 21t, DgDigital 4, FabrikaSimf 9t, Dmitry Finkel 5t, Jeni Foto 16, Gelpi 6, Inside Creative House 10, Knelson20 21c, LumenSt 9b, J Main 19, Tetiana Rostopira 28l, Luke Schmidt 24, solarseven 25, Withan Tor 26-27, You Touch pix of EuToch 22.

All other artworks and photographs © Brown Bear Books.

Cataloging-in-Publication Data

Names: O'Daly, Anne.
Title: Measuring volume / Anne O'Daly.
Description: New York : Powerkids Press, 2024. | Series: Measure it with math! | Includes glossary and index.
Identifiers: ISBN 9781642827910 (pbk.) | ISBN 9781642827927 (library bound) | ISBN 9781642827934 (ebook)
Subjects: LCSH: Volume (Cubic content)--Juvenile literature. | Volume perception--Juvenile literature. | Measurement--Juvenile literature.
Classification: LCC QC104.O34 2024 | DDC 530.8--dc23

Manufactured in the United States of America

CPSIA Compliance Information: Batch #CSPK24. For further information contact Rosen Publishing at 1-800-237-9932.

Contents

What Is Volume? 4
Changing Size 6
What Are Units? 8
Liquid Volumes 10
Metric Measurements 12
Finding the Volume 14
Spheres and Cones 16
Harder Shapes 18
Take a Guess 20
Amazing Water 22
Heat and Volume 24
Huge Volumes 26
  HANDS ON:
Equal Volumes? 28
Glossary 30
Find Out More 31
Index and Answers 32

What Is Volume?

The Airbus Beluga is one of the biggest airplanes ever built. It carries large pieces of aircraft and bulky vehicles. The airplane has enough space inside to fit about 50,000 basketballs. A Boeing 747 is another large airplane. It carries more than 350 passengers. A 747 plane could fit around 30,000 basketballs. A sport utility vehicle is much smaller. It can hold around 75 basketballs.

The *Symphony of the Seas* cruise ship could carry about 80,000,000 basketballs.

FACT

The world's largest cruise ship is called the Symphony of the Seas. It can carry 6,988 passengers.

The amount of space something can hold is called its volume. An Airbus Beluga has more volume than a 747 because it can hold more things. A sport utility vehicle has less volume than a 747. It can hold fewer things.

The Beluga airbus is named for a type of whale. It is used to carry huge pieces of equipment, including large airplane parts.

We can think of volume another way. Volume is the amount of space something takes up. Fifty thousand basketballs take up a certain volume. That volume is the same as the volume or space inside an Airbus Beluga.

COMPARING VOLUMES

We can measure a volume by finding out how many times a smaller volume fits inside it. We do this when we say that an airplane holds 50,000 basketballs. We are measuring the airplane's volume by comparing it with the volume of a basketball.

> 1 basketball x 50,000
> = 1 Airbus Beluga airplane

Changing Size

The volume of an object depends on the object's size. The bigger the object, the more it can hold. A longer airplane usually has more volume than a shorter one. If we could make the airplane wider or higher, that would make the volume bigger, too.

Volume is also linked to area. Area is the size of a flat surface. If we made the size of an airplane's floor bigger, but kept its height the same, the volume would increase.

When we blow up a party balloon, its length doesn't increase by much, but its volume increases a lot.

THREE DIMENSIONS

Length is a measurement in one direction. Sometimes we call this direction a dimension. To measure an area, we usually have to measure both its length and width. So area is a measurement in two directions, or dimensions. To find something's volume, we have to measure it in three directions. So, volume is a measurement in three dimensions: length, height, and width.

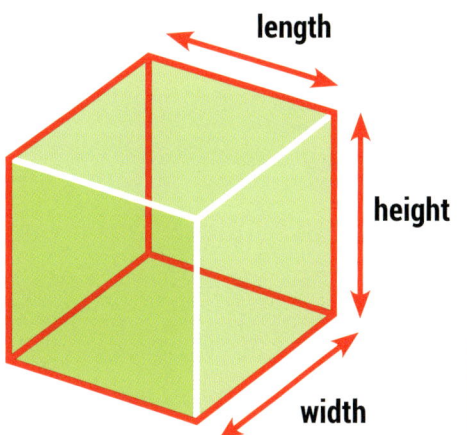

Area = width x height
Volume = width x height x length

Changing Volumes

Length, area, and volume are linked. Making one of these things bigger usually makes all the others bigger, too. However, this is not always true.

For example, we could make an airplane just a little bit longer but only half as high and half as wide. Even though it was longer, that airplane would have less volume inside.

FACT
The first balloon was made by scientist Michael Faraday in 1824. He was famous for his discoveries about electricity.

What Are Units?

When we measure the length of something, we give the answer in feet and inches. These are called units. Units tell us what we are measuring. They can be grouped together to make a system. Feet and inches are part of the imperial system. This system is used in the United States.

TRY THIS

ESTIMATING VOLUMES

You can estimate the volume of a sphere such as a junior basketball by fitting it inside an imaginary cube. An estimate is a good guess. The cube must be a tight fit around the ball. The cube around this basketball is 9 inches long, tall, and wide. The cube will always have a larger volume than the sphere it holds.

length x height x width = volume

What is the volume of the cube?

Can you estimate the volume of the ball?

Answers on page 32.

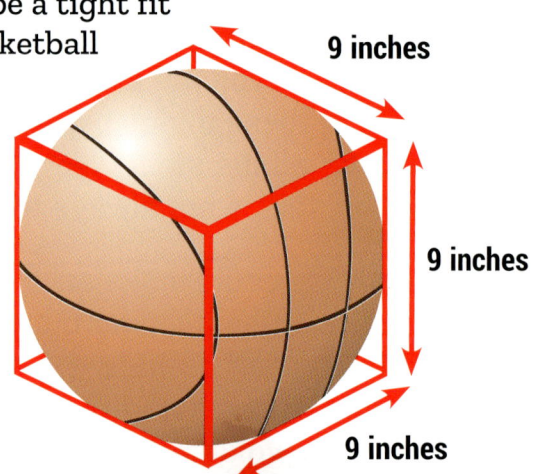

CUBIC UNITS

1 cubic foot
= 12 inches x 12 inches x 12 inches
= 1,728 cubic inches

1 cubic yard, or 27 cubic feet
= 36 inches x 36 inches x 36 inches
= 46,656 cubic inches

1 cubic mile
= 1,760 yards x 1,760 yards x 1,760 yards
= 5½ billion cubic yards

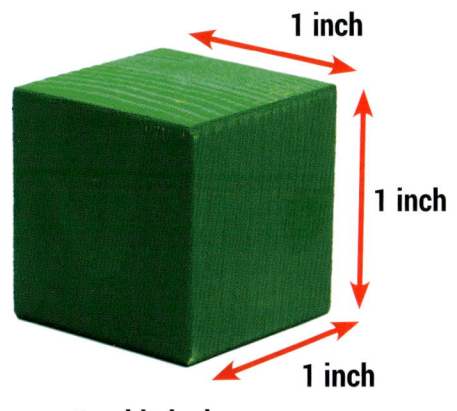

1 cubic inch

Volume also has units. Think about measuring the volume of a cube. The cube measures 1 foot long by 1 foot wide by 1 foot high. Its volume is 1 cubic foot. A cubic foot is a volume measuring 1 foot in each direction.

Small and Large Units

Each unit of length has a matching unit of volume. We can measure small volumes in cubic inches. A cubic inch measures 1 inch long by 1 inch wide by 1 inch high. We can measure larger volumes in cubic yards or cubic miles.

The volume of this lunchbox is around 72 cubic inches. The volume inside a sport utility vehicle is about 150 cubic feet.

Liquid Volumes

Volume is the amount of space inside a shape. We also measure the volume of liquids. Liquid volume tells us how much space the liquid takes up. Liquid volumes have their own units. When an adult fills a car's tank with gasoline, the liquid is measured in gallons. Milk comes in pints and quarts.

Smaller volumes are used for cooking. These are fluid ounces. Gallons, quarts, pints, and fluid ounces are all part of the imperial system for measuring.

This woman is using a jug to measure out a healthy smoothie.

VOLUME OR CAPACITY?

Volume and capacity are different things. Suppose you have two jugs. One can hold 1 pint, the other can hold 2 pints. They have different capacities. Now think about pouring milk into the jugs. If you pour ½ pint of liquid into each of the jugs, the capacities are different but the volume of liquid is the same. Capacity is the amount a container can hold. Volume is how much liquid is in the container.

These containers all have the same capacity. But they are holding different volumes of liquids.

TRY THIS

1 gallon = 4 quarts
1 quart = 2 pints
1 pint = 16 fluid ounces

* How many fluid ounces are in a quart?
* How many fluid ounces are in a gallon?

Answers on page 32.

FACT

A gallon is about the same volume as 230 cubic inches.

Metric Measurements

Imperial measures are used in the United States. In other parts of the world, people use a different set of measures. These are metric measures. Metric measurements for length include centimeters, meters, and kilometers. There are 100 centimeters in a meter and 1,000 meters in a kilometer.

The metric system also has cubic units. Small volumes are measured in cubic millimeters or cubic centimeters. Larger volumes are measured in cubic meters or cubic kilometers.

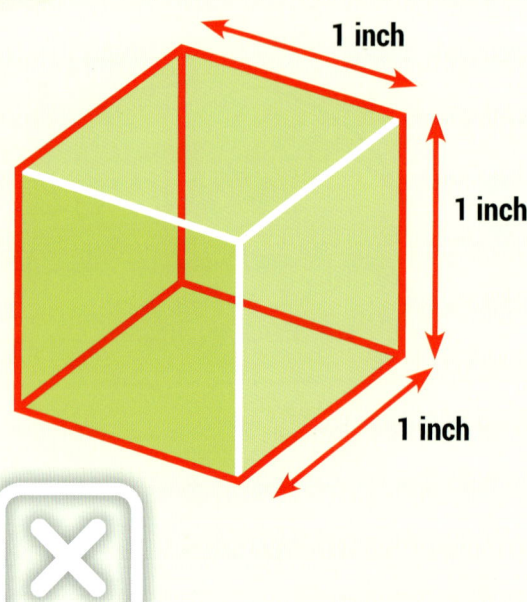

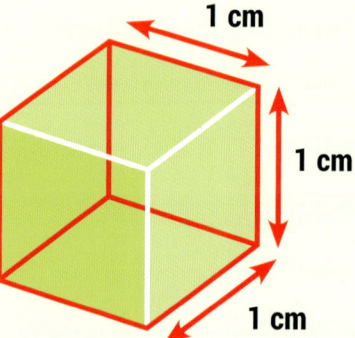

The larger cube has a volume of 1 cubic inch, which is an imperial unit. The smaller cube has a volume of 1 cubic centimeter. This is a metric unit.

Liquid Measures

There are common liquid measures in the metric system, too. A liter is about the same size as a pint and three-fourths, or about a fourth, of a gallon. Drinks can be measured in liters. There are a thousand milliliters in a liter. A teaspoon can hold about 5 milliliters.

This jug holds about 2 liters (4 pints) of milk. The glass holds about half a liter (about a pint).

TRY THIS

Convert the missing **?** measurements:

DRY MEASURES:
imperial to metric
1 cubic inch = 16 cubic centimeters
1 cubic foot = $3/100$ cubic meter
1 cubic yard = ¾ cubic meter
1 cubic mile = 4 cubic kilometers

metric to imperial
1 cubic centimeter = $6/100$ cubic inch
1 cubic meter = **?** cubic feet
1 cubic meter = $1 1/3$ cubic yards
1 cubic kilometer = ¼ cubic mile

LIQUID MEASURES:
imperial to metric
1 fluid ounce = 30 milliliters
1 pint = **?** liter or 500 milliliters
1 quart = **?** liter or 1,000 milliliters
1 gallon = **?** liters

metric to imperial
1 milliliter = $3/100$ fluid ounces
1 liter = 34 fluid ounces
1 liter = **?** pints
1 liter = **?** gallon

Answers on page 32.

Finding the Volume

It's easy to find the volume of a simple object, like a box or a cube. We just need to measure the object in three different directions. The simplest volume we can measure is the volume of a box.

Three Directions
The volume of a box is its length times its height times its width. A cube is a simple box shape. Its length, height, and width are all the same. If the length of the cube is measured in inches, the volume is measured in cubic inches.

It's easy to find the volume of a box. You just need to measure the height, length, and width.

Pyramid Volume

Ancient Egyptians built pyramids. The shape may look tricky, but it's easy to work out the volume of a pyramid.

Three pyramids with a square base fit inside a cube. To find the volume of a pyramid, we figure out the length x length x height. Then we divide the answer by three.

The volume of a cube, or a square-sided box = length x height x width.

The volume of a pyramid with a square base = $\frac{1}{3}$ x length x length x height.

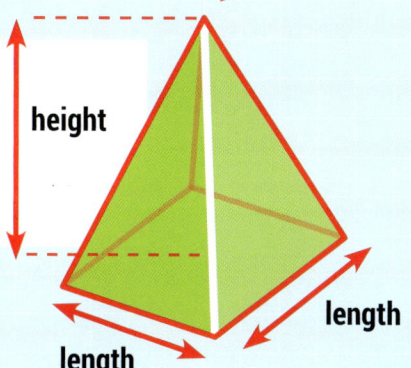

TRY THIS

FIND THE VOLUME OF A ROOM

Choose a room in your house that is box shaped. Use a ruler or tape measure to find the length and the width of the room, to the nearest number of feet. Ask an adult to help you measure the height.

To find the volume of the room, multiply the length by the height, and then multiply that number by the width. The number you get is the volume of the room. It will be measured in cubic feet.

Spheres and Cones

It is harder to measure round and curved objects. But we can find their volume. All we need is something called pi! Pi is a special number. It has its own symbol, so we sometimes see it written like this, π. Pi means the number 3.141. It helps us find curved volumes.

Volumes of Spheres

Spheres are round shapes, like soccer balls and oranges. You can use a formula to figure out the volume of a sphere if you know its radius. (The radius is the distance from the sphere's center to the outside.) That formula is:

Volume of sphere =
1.33 x pi x radius x radius x radius

The radius of this sphere, right, is 1 inch. So, its volume is:

      1.33 x pi x 1 x 1 x 1
        = about 4 cubic inches (4 in³)
     (4.18 in³ more accurately)

These tasty treats have a sphere of ice cream in a cone, with a cylinder cookie. We can figure out the volumes of all the shapes using the special number, pi.

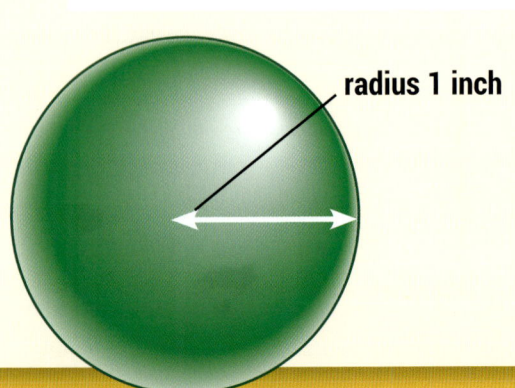

radius 1 inch

Volumes of Cones

There are also formulas for figuring out the volume of more complicated shapes, such as cones and cylinders:

Volume of cone =
0.33 x pi x radius x radius x height of cone

The radius of this cone, right, is 1 inch. The cone is 2.5 inches tall. So, its volume is:

> 0.33 x pi x 1 x 1 x 2.5
> = 2.5 cubic inches (2.5 in^3)
> (2.59 in^3 more accurately)

Volume of cylinder =
pi x radius x radius x height of cylinder

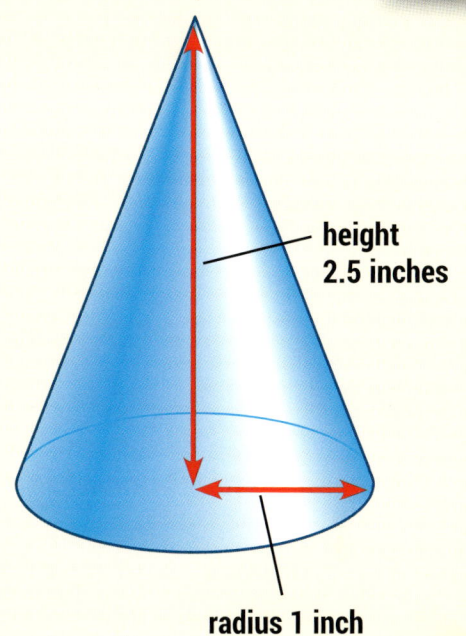

height 2.5 inches

radius 1 inch

TRY THIS

VOLUME OF A CYLINDER

Can you figure out the volume of this cylinder? Remember:

pi x radius x radius x height = volume

Answer on page 32.

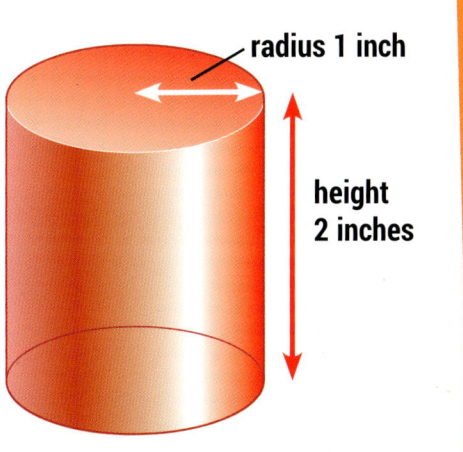

radius 1 inch

height 2 inches

Harder Shapes

Not all objects have simple shapes. How do we find their volume? By taking them apart! A dome is half of a sphere. Its volume is equal to the volume of a sphere divided by two. A pencil is a bit like a cone stuck to a cylinder.

Added Together
We can always find the volume of an object by trying to find simpler objects inside it. We can figure out the volume of each of these simple objects. Then we can add their volumes together to find the volume of the whole object. So the volume of the object is the volume of the parts added together.

These more complicated objects can be broken down into a cube plus a square-based pyramid (left) and a cylinder plus a cone (right). Then it is easy to figure out the total volume of each object.

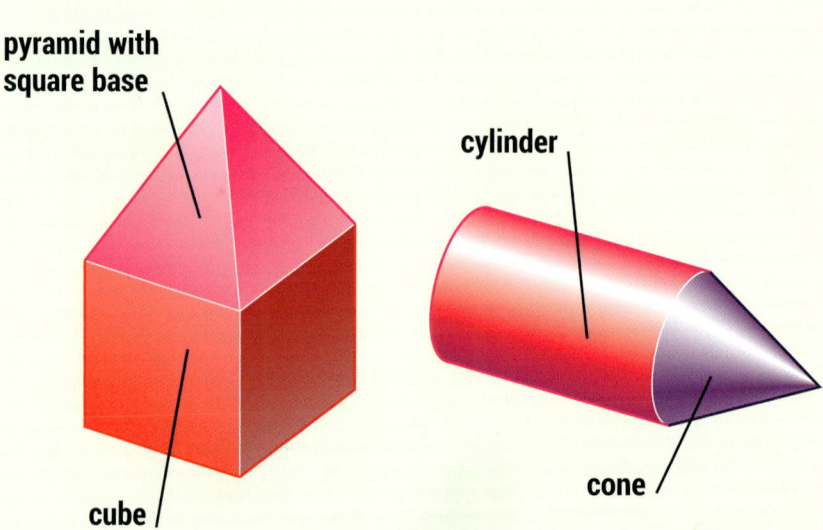

VOLUME OF THE CAPITOL

Suppose you wanted to find out the volume of the U.S. Capitol in Washington, D.C. If you look closely, you can see that the building is made up of a dome, sitting on a cylinder, which sits on several boxes. A dome is a sphere cut in half. So the volume of the Capitol is half the volume of a sphere, plus the volume of the cylinder, plus the volume of the boxes beneath the cylinder.

The cylinder under the dome of the Capitol is called the Rotunda. Its volume is 1.3 million cubic feet.

Take a Guess

How can we find the volume of something that is hard to measure? It's hard to measure Earth, but we can guess its volume. Imagine an enormous box that is big enough to hold Earth inside it. If we could measure the volume of the box, that would tell us roughly how big Earth is. But Earth would fit inside the box with room to spare. So our measurement of volume is only really a good guess. We call a measurement like that an estimate.

If we could fit Earth inside a huge box, then the volume of the box would give us an estimate of the volume of Earth. The box would be larger than Earth, of course.

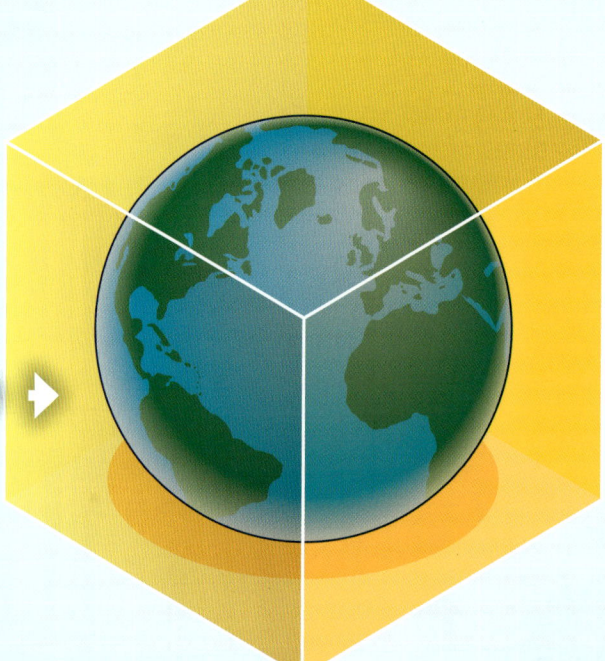

VOLUME OF OCEANS

The Atlantic Ocean has an area of about 41 million square miles (106 million square kilometers). It is about 2 miles (3.5 kilometers) deep. We can estimate the volume of the Atlantic Ocean by multiplying these two numbers. That gives a volume of 85 million cubic miles (355 million cubic kilometers). The ocean has different depths in different places, so the answer is only an estimate.

Atlantic Ocean

Making an Estimate

An estimate is sometimes the best measurement we can make. An example of an estimate is explaining the volume of an airplane by saying how many basketballs would fit inside it. The basketballs do not fill up the plane completely. There are spaces between the balls. When we say a 747 airplane holds 30,000 basketballs, that is an estimate of the airplane's volume. It is not an exact measurement.

Amazing Water

Water is everywhere. It is in the oceans, in the air, and in the ground. Without water, no animals or plants could survive on Earth. Like many other substances, water can be a solid, a liquid, or a gas.

The same amount of water takes up different volumes when it is ice, water, or steam. When water freezes into ice, it takes up more volume. When ice melts back into water, it takes up less room. Hot water takes up more volume than cold water. Steam spreads out to take up the most volume of all.

The water inside this bottle froze to become ice. But ice takes up more volume than water. The glass bottle could not hold the ice, so the glass broke.

Making Steam

When water is boiled in a kettle or pan, it makes clouds of steam. A small amount of water seems to make a lot of steam. As the steam cools down, it changes back to liquid. It takes up less space.

We can also make the volume of steam smaller by squeezing it. That pushes the steam particles closer together.

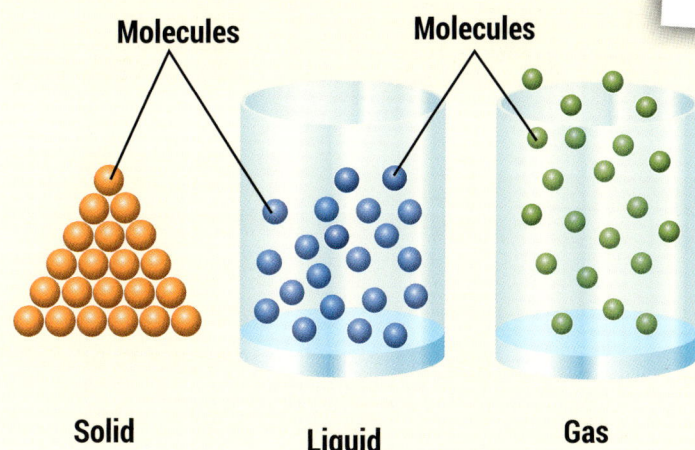

Solid   Liquid   Gas

Everything is made up of tiny invisible particles called atoms. Atoms join to form molecules. The molecules in a solid are packed closely together. The molecules in a liquid spread out to the shape of the container. The molecules in a gas spread out as far as they can. So a gas takes up the most volume.

AEROGELS

Aerogels are special materials that were invented in the 1930s. They are solids, but most of the volume they take up is air, so they weigh almost nothing. Aerogels are light and strong. They have lots of different uses. One is to make very warm and very light clothes. Another is to make windows that trap the heat.

Heat and Volume

The volume of a material changes when we heat it. If you put a glass of cold water in sunshine, the heat makes the water molecules move around more. The molecules take up more space. So hot water takes up more volume than cold water because it expands, or grows larger.

EXPLOSIVE VOLUMES

Substances such as gunpowder and dynamite are explosives. When an explosive is heated, it changes from a solid to a gas. Gases expand very quickly and make huge volumes. Explosives take up very little volume to start with. But the gas they make takes up much more volume. As the gas is produced, it can make a big explosion which can blow out windows or even knock down large buildings.

Explosives are used to knock down buildings. The explosion is controlled to make sure no one is hurt and no other buildings are damaged.

Amazing firework displays like this are caused by chemical reactions. The reactions create chemicals with larger volumes.

Stretching Volumes

You sometimes see power lines stretching lower in the summer. The heat makes the metal wires expand and take up more volume. Metal doors heat up and expand in the summer. That makes them hard to open and close. Even a huge building like the U.S. Capitol expands slightly in hot weather. It takes up very slightly more volume in summer than in winter!

Chemical Changes

Volumes can change during a chemical reaction. That is what happens when we mix chemicals together. We make new chemicals that take up more volume than the ones we started with. Chemical reactions make fireworks explode.

FACT

The most powerful fireworks can shoot 1,300 feet (400 meters) into the sky.

Huge Volumes

Some volumes are enormous! Earth is part of the solar system, which is made of the sun and eight planets. Planet Earth has a volume of about 260 billion cubic miles (1 trillion cubic kilometers). The biggest planet is Jupiter. More than 1,300 Earths would fit into Jupiter. The smallest planet is Mercury. About 18 Mercurys would fit inside Earth.

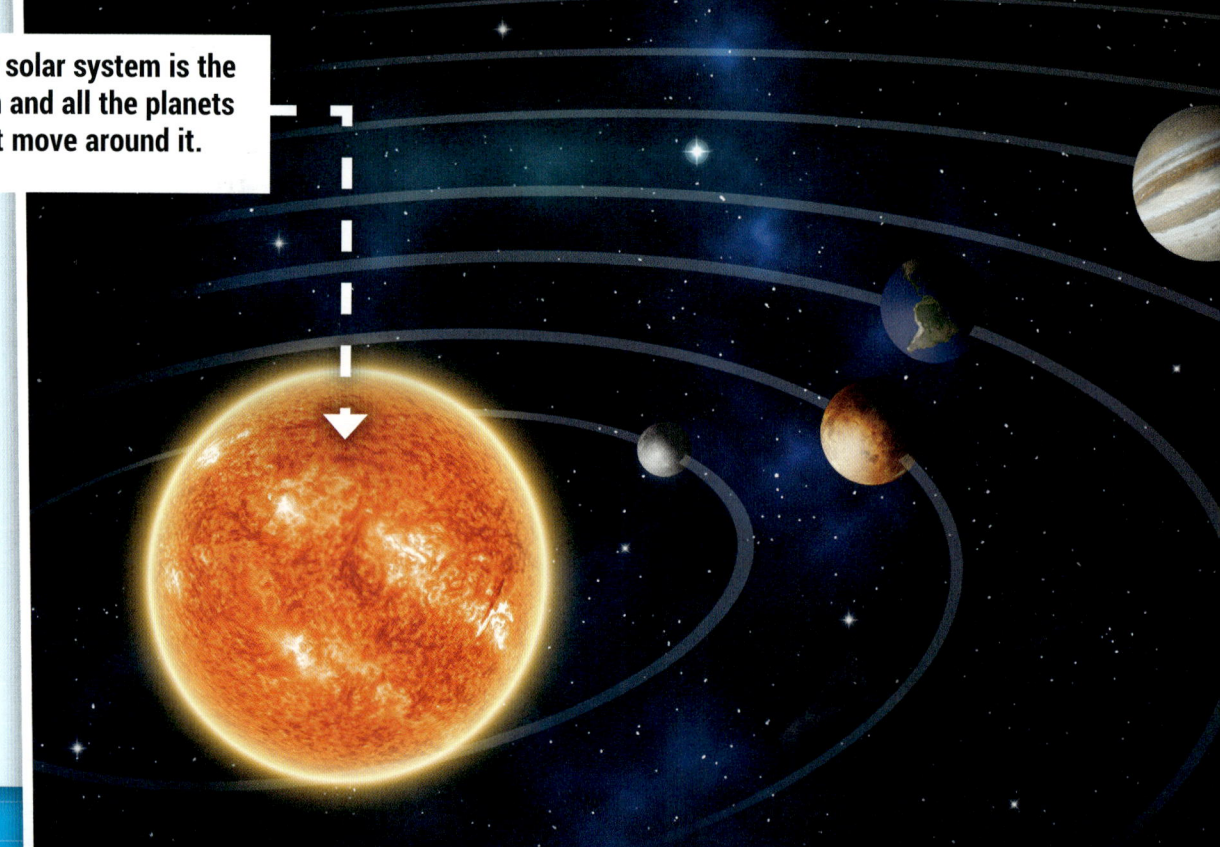

Our solar system is the Sun and all the planets that move around it.

The biggest object in our solar system is the sun. It could fit 1.3 million Earths inside it! The sun is a star. Some stars are much bigger. A star called Betelgeuse has hundreds of millions of times more volume than the sun.

Our solar system is just one part of the universe. Everything in space, including planets, solar systems, and stars, is called the universe. No one knows how big the universe is. It is expanding (getting bigger) all the time, so its volume is always getting bigger.

WATER EVERYWHERE

Earth contains 330 million cubic miles (about 1,300 million cubic kilometers) of water! Much of it is frozen as ice near the North and South Poles. Climate change is heating the planet and making the ice melt. If all that ice melted, the volume of the oceans would increase enormously. The sea level would rise. Many of our towns and cities would be flooded.

HANDS ON
Equal Volumes?

WHAT YOU NEED

* Modeling clay
* Two rulers
* Pen and paper

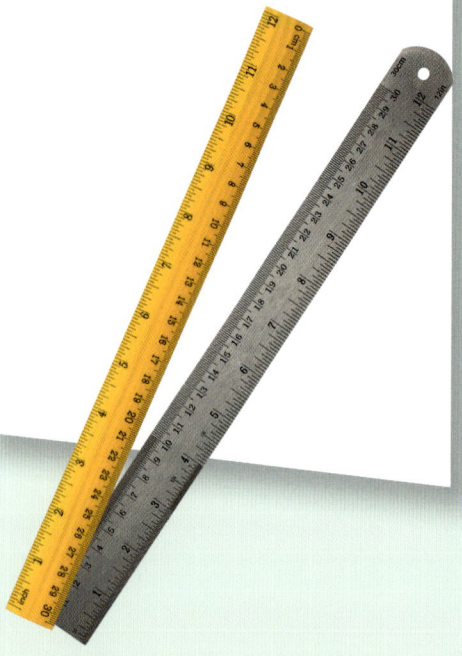

WHAT YOU DO

1. First, make the modeling clay into a cube. A cube is as tall as it is wide and long. It is easier to make a cube if you first roll the clay into a ball. Make sure the ball is not oval (like a small football). It should be round (like a small tennis ball).

2. Squeeze the ball of modeling clay between the flat sides of two rulers to make all the sides of your cube flat.

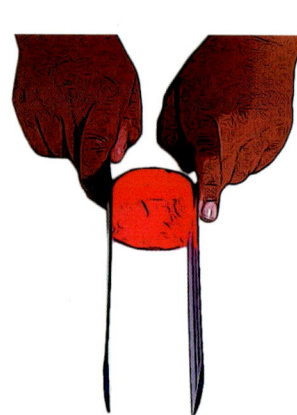

This May Help

Sometimes the modeling clay may stick to the rulers and pull your cube apart. Try spraying a little cooking oil on the rulers before you start to squeeze the clay. This usually stops the clay from sticking to the rulers.

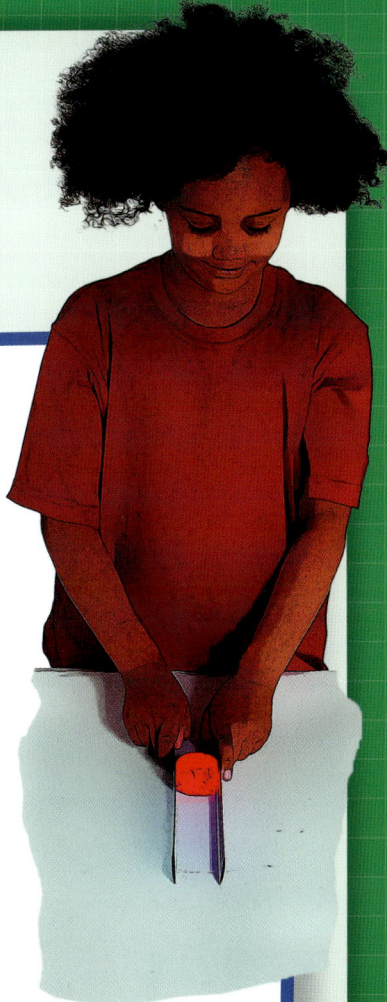

3. Measure the length, width, and height of your cube. These measurements should all be the same on a cube. Keep molding and measuring the clay until you have an exact cube.

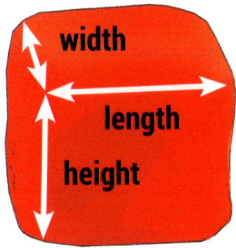

4. When you have an exact cube, measure the length, width, and height in inches. Write these measurements down. Then use this sum to figure out your cube's volume:

length x width x height = volume

Because you measured the cube in inches, the volume will be in cubic inches. Make sure you write "cubic inches" after the answer.

5. Make your cube into a longer box shape. Squeeze it between the two rulers to make the sides flat. Do not add or take away any clay.

6. Repeat step **4** to calculate the volume of your new shape.

7. Compare the volumes of your two shapes. The two measurements should be the same. The cube and the box are different shapes, but they have the same volume.

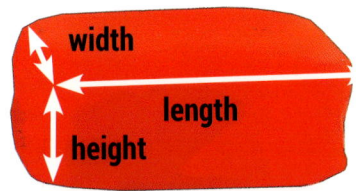

Glossary

area The amount of space that a surface takes up.

cube A box-shaped object.

cubic foot A volume measuring one foot long by one foot high by one foot wide.

cubic inch A volume measuring one inch in each direction.

cubic meter A volume measuring one meter in each direction.

cubic mile A volume measuring one mile in each direction.

cubic unit A unit for measuring volumes.

dimension A direction in which we measure something. Lengths are measured in one dimension, areas in two dimensions, and volumes in three dimensions.

distance The length between two points.

estimate A rough measurement; sometimes just a good guess.

expand The way in which something gets bigger.

fluid ounce A small measurement of liquid volume.

gallon A measurement of volume.

imperial A system for measuring things, which includes pints, quarts, and gallons.

liter A metric measurement of volume equal to a quarter of a gallon.

metric A system for measuring things. A liter is a metric measurement.

pi A special number used to work out areas and volumes with curves. Pi has the value 3.141 and is often written with the Greek symbol π.

reaction In chemistry, something that happens when two different substances are added together.

unit A measurement of something. Examples of volume units are cubic inches, pints, gallons, and liters.

Find Out More

BOOKS

Askew, Mike.
Let's Measure It. You Can Master Math.
Rosen Publishing, 2022.

Jones, Christianne.
Measuring At Home.
Capstone Publishing, 2019.

Murray, Julie.
Measure It! Volume.
Abdo Kids Junior, 2019.

Rustad, Martha E.
Measuring Volume.
Capstone Publishing, 2019.

WEBSITES

www.sciencemadesimple.com/volume_conversion.php
Convert volumes from imperial to metric and from metric to imperial.

kids.kiddle.co/Volume
This website has information about volume, units of volume, and how to measure it.

www.bbc.co.uk/bitesize/topics/zjbg87h/articles/zrdcbqt
Find out about volume and capacity, with simple examples and a quiz.

Publisher's note to educators and parents: Our editors have carefully reviewed these websites to ensure that they are suitable for students. Many websites change frequently, however, and we cannot guarantee that a site's future contents will continue to meet our high standards of quality and educational value. Be advised that students should be closely supervised whenever they access the Internet.

Index

aerogel 23
airplane 4, 5, 6, 7, 21
area 6, 7, 21
Atlantic Ocean 21
atom 23
basketball 4, 5, 8, 21
box 9, 14, 15, 19, 20, 29
Capitol Building 19, 25
centimeter 12, 13
chemicals 25
cone 16, 17, 18
cube 8, 9, 12, 14, 15, 18, 28, 29
cubic centimeter 12, 13
cubic foot 9, 13, 15, 19
cubic inch 9, 11, 12, 13, 14, 16, 17, 29
cubic kilometer 12, 13, 21, 26, 27
cubic meter 12, 13
cubic mile 9, 13, 21, 26, 27
cubic millimeter 12
cubic yard 9, 13
curved volumes 16, 17

cylinder 16, 17, 18, 19
dimension 7
dome 18, 19
Earth 20, 22, 26, 27
estimate 8, 20, 21
explosives 24
fireworks 25
floods 27
fluid ounce 10, 12, 13
foot 8, 12, 15, 25
formula 16, 17
gallon 10, 11, 13
gas 22, 23, 24
height 6, 7, 8, 14, 15, 17, 29
ice 22, 27
imperial units 8, 10, 12, 13
inch 9, 11, 12, 13, 14, 16, 17, 29
kilometer 12, 13, 21, 26, 27
length 6, 7, 8, 12, 14, 15, 29
liquid 10, 11, 13, 22, 23

liter 13
meter 12, 13, 25
metric measures 12, 13
metric volume 12, 13
mile 9, 13, 21, 26, 27
milliliter 13
molecule 23, 24
pi 16, 17
pint 10, 11, 12, 13
pyramid 15, 18
quart 10, 11, 12, 13
radius 16, 17
sea level 27
solid 22, 23, 24
South Pole 27
space 4, 5, 10, 21, 23, 24, 25
sphere 8, 16, 17, 18, 19
square pyramid 15, 18
steam 22, 23
universe 27
water 22, 23, 24, 27
width 6, 7, 8, 14, 15, 29

ANSWERS

Page 8: 729 cubic inches; the basketball has a smaller volume. **Page 11:** 32 fluid ounces; 128 fluid ounces. **Page 13:** 35 cubic feet; about ½ liter; about 1 liter; about 4 liters; 1¾ pints; ¼ gallon. **Page 17:** 6.28 cubic inches.